PREACHERS' HANDBOOK

SERMON OUTLINES FOR 2000

based on

the IBRA Bible readings in

Words for Today and *Light for our Path*

INTERNATIONAL BIBLE READING ASSOCIATION

Cover photograph:

The Centre for Black and White Christian Partnership,
Selly Oak, Birmingham

Editor – Kate Hughes

Published by:
The International Bible Reading Association
1020 Bristol Road
Selly Oak
Birmingham B29 6LB
Great Britain

ISBN 0-7197-0939-3
ISSN 0140-8267

Typeset by International Bible Reading Association
Printed and bound in Malta by
Halcyon Print & Design

CONTENTS

Introduction
Abbreviations and Acknowledgements

INTRODUCTION

Dear Friends

Welcome to this year's *Preachers' Handbook*. The sermon outlines are based on the scheme of Bible reading notes used in *Light for our Path* and *Words for Today*. However, it is not necessary to have read the daily Bible notes in order to make use of the same themes and readings in *Preachers' Handbook*, and for the first time this year we have listed the sermon outlines by weeks of the year, as well as by a specific date in the year 2000. We hope that this will give the book a longer useful life, as a resource and reference book.

Although I am not ordained, I preach regularly in my local Anglican church, and find that preparing and delivering sermons can build up my own faith (I hope it does the same for my hearers!). But sometimes I cannot think of anything to say on the set Bible readings, and then I am grateful for advice and ideas from other, more experienced, preachers. It seems to me that *Preachers' Handbook* can fulfil these two functions:

- it can build up your faith as you exchange ideas with other Christians and learn from their experience of God;

- and it can help you with ideas at those times (which come to all of us) when your mind goes blank or pastoral demands swamp the time needed to prepare a sermon.

On both these counts, I hope that you will find *Preachers' Handbook* a valuable resource.

Kate Hughes
Editor

ABBREVIATIONS AND ACKNOWLEDGEMENTS

We are grateful for permission to quote from the following Bible versions:

GNB   *Good News Bible*, 4th edition, published by The Bible Societies/HarperCollins, © American Bible Society, 1976.

NIV   *The Holy Bible, New International Version*, Copyright © 1973, 1978, 1984 by International Bible Society. Used by permission of Hodder & Stoughton Ltd., a member of the Hodder Headline Plc Group. All rights reserved. 'NIV' is a registered trademark of International Bible Society. UK trademark no. 1448790.

NJB   *The New Jerusalem Bible*, published by Darton, Longman & Todd, © Darton, Longman & Todd Ltd and Doubleday & Company, Inc., 1985.

NRSV   *New Revised Standard Version Bible*, published by HarperCollins, © Division of Christian Education of the National Council of the Churches of Christ in the United States of America, 1989.

RSV   *The Holy Bible, Revised Standard Version*, published by Thomas Nelson & Sons, © Division of Christian Education of the National Council of the Churches of Christ in the United States of America, 1952.

Vision

Text: Then the one who sits on the throne said, 'And now I make all things new!'

(Revelation 21.5, GNB)

AIM
To encourage people to be forward-looking in their Christian lives.

Sermon notes by
David Huggett

based on readings for
Week 1
(January 2 - 8,
2000)

Introduction
Tunnel vision is a medical condition which is both distressing and potentially dangerous. It can also be a spiritual condition which makes us ineffective, because it distorts God's purposes for us. We need to be focused in our Christian faith but, like the photographer, it should be with a 'wide angle' lens.

● **We should focus on the past.** Don't live in the past, but at the same time don't ignore it. The Israelites were acutely conscious of their remarkable history, and learnt many lessons from it. The Millennium is a time for celebrating the past and reflecting upon our Christian heritage.

● **We should focus on the future.** Think of some of the new things you have received recently. Or think of that new job, or new relationship, or new baby, or new challenge that you hope for. Newness brings excitement. God gives us many opportunities to make a new beginning, but there is none more exciting than being in at the start of a new Millennium. Grateful for what is past, we can face forward to something much bigger and wider than simply a new day, or even a new year.

● **We should focus on God.** But the Millennium is above all a Christian celebration, and so God should be at its centre. Our text reminds us that 'I make all things new.' Many of the celebrations will last just a few hours. The challenge for us is to see the vision that God can be at the centre whatever happens in the future.

'Stay focused on God'

Conclusion If we focus on God, then all the rest will come into proper perspective.

To the preacher. Take time in your personal preparation to celebrate your own history in the light of your calling to serve God, and re-commit your future service to him.

Repentance

Sermon notes by
Judith Rossall

*based on
readings for
Week 2
(January 9 – 15, 2000)*

*'God looks
forward'*

Text: **'I tell you that in the same way there will be more rejoicing in heaven over one sinner who repents than over ninety-nine righteous persons who do not need to repent.'**
(Luke 15.7, NIV Inclusive Language Edition)

AIM
To encourage people to see repentance as a positive part of their discipleship.

Introduction
We begin with an invitation to a party. What are we celebrating? A birth, a wedding, an anniversary? No — this party is a celebration with God because a sinner has repented.

● **What kind of God?** Most of us see repentance as a very negative thing. The idea of God rejoicing over our repentance can be very difficult — is this a cruel God who likes to be proved right? Many of our problems in the Christian life stem from a bad image of God; unless we really believe in God's love it is very difficult to trust God. To put repentance in context we need to look at Jesus' image of God as a loving heavenly Father.

● **A loving Father rejoices.** Perhaps one of the reasons why we see repentance as a negative thing is because for us it is about looking backwards. I got that wrong. I'm a bad person and repentance makes me feel bad about myself. Perhaps God rejoices over our repentance because God looks forward. Repentance means a relationship renewed, a sinner restored and a chance to do better in future.

Conclusion Many Christians today have lost the old art of self-examination and repentance. We need to understand that every time we truly repent we draw a little closer to God — and that is something over which we can truly rejoice.

To the preacher. Think about your congregation: if they tend to emphasize the joy and victory of following Christ, they may need help to think about what repentance means for them. Other congregations may need more emphasis on the love of God and the joy of drawing closer to God.

Following

Text: You hem me in, behind and before, and lay your hand upon me. **(Psalm 139.5, NRSV)**

Sermon notes by
Valerie Ogden

based on readings for
Week 3
(January 16–22, 2000)

AIM
To help people reflect on and appreciate God's presence and God's call.

Introduction
Highlight negative and positive experiences of being 'hemmed in' or unable to escape. The frustration of the nose-to-tail traffic jam — and the lovers' embrace from which neither wants to escape. (Think of your own examples.) According to the Psalmist, there is no escape from God.

● **You hem me in behind and before.** The Hebrew mind had a strong sense of Yahweh moving before and behind his people (see *Exodus 14.19ff*). Is this idea also helpful to us? Have we been aware of Christ's presence going before us into a challenging situation — or staying behind us to cushion us when we fall? Illustrate from personal experience if possible.

● **And lay your hand upon me.** The God who is behind and before us also lays his hand upon us. In some ordination services, especially in large African churches,

'God behind and before us'

the one to be ordained kneels and is literally 'hemmed in' by the bodies of other clergy. This can make the ordinand feel quite trapped. But when hands are laid on the ordinand's head, the purpose of the closed circle becomes clear. We are within God's protection when he calls and commissions us to do his work and lays his hands upon us to equip us. (Develop the idea of God surrounding us from all sides, but at the same time commissioning us to take risks.)

Conclusion We reaffirm our belief that God is inescapable and recommit ourselves to respond to him whenever his hand touches us.

To the preacher. Amos 9 could provide an additional but demanding angle on the theme. In this sermon, guard against presenting God's presence as some kind of divine insurance policy: e.g., if God is surrounding us, nothing can go wrong. This is both dangerous and unbiblical.

Proclaiming good news

Sermon notes by
Allen Smith

based on readings for
Week 4
(January 23 – 29, 2000)

'Check in with Jesus'

Text: 'The time has come,' [Jesus] said. 'The kingdom of God is near. Repent and believe the good news!' (Mark 1.15, NIV)

AIM
To encourage an active response to the gospel of Jesus Christ.

Introduction
The good news that Jesus proclaims is his saving purpose: a promise of victory over sin and new life under God's eternal rule for those who repent, believe and follow Jesus.

● **Repent.** Airlines insist that passengers check in on time and restrict the amount of personal luggage. Journeying with Jesus means being ready to leave when he calls and abandon excess baggage: heavy burdens, selfish needs and possessions which hinder our progress. The airport detection system picks up anything which might endanger the flight; in the same way we need to recognize and deal with sin before we can enjoy our journey with Jesus. Repentance is more than feeling guilty and sorry. Repentance is unloading the weight of sin, ready to soar through the clouds.

● **Believe.** When we begin a journey, we are usually confident that we shall reach our destination. Yet in life, we often seem to go round in circles, without any real purpose. Jesus came to proclaim the good news and to show the way by his obedience to his Father's will. Those who believe in him can travel with Jesus into the kingdom.

● **Follow.** The pilot guides a plane through turbulence and stormy weather. We cannot just get off when the journey gets difficult. We have to trust the pilot — and trust Jesus — to bring us safely to our destination.

Conclusion Jesus plots our course and takes care of us along the way until we reach the place he has prepared for us. So we can trust him, check in and enjoy the journey.

To the preacher. Consider sharing your own Christian journey of faith, the 'baggage' you had to leave behind and the joys of the journey.

Opposing evil

Text: 'I will put my words in his mouth.'
(Deuteronomy 18.18, RSV)

Sermon notes by
Philip Wadham
based on readings for
Week 5
(January 30 –
February 5, 2000)

AIM
To help people recognize that God's truth is still proclaimed by prophets.

Introduction
Limiting the biblical prophets to foretelling the future is too narrow. Their primary role is to proclaim God's will clearly to the people.

● **Liberating action.** Moses, the first of the prophets, demanded that Pharaoh, king of Egypt, 'let God's people

'Are there prophets among us?'

go', liberating them from slavery. His call came directly from God and Moses obeyed *(Exodus 3)*. This liberating God has called prophets throughout history to the same task. (Give some examples of prophets who obeyed the call and worked hard to liberate people, both on the world scene — Martin Luther King, Bishop Oscar Romero, etc. — and local figures. Avoid spiritualizing 'liberation'.)

● **Local action.** Over the centuries, as the story was frequently retold, the Exodus took on spectacular proportions, involving thousands of people. The actual event was probably much more modest: a small group of people escaping slavery under the direction of a God-inspired leader. (God's concern for justice is both local and global. In reality, most prophets are called to local action.)

● **Reaction.** Neither Moses nor his successor Joshua had an easy time. First Pharaoh, then their own people reacted against them. Moses called Joshua to 'Be strong, stand firm ... do not be disheartened by anything' *(Deuteronomy 31.7)*. It is easy to get disheartened. Moses' advice is not always easy to put into practice. (Again, give examples, preferably from something that touches you deeply.)

Conclusion Prophets are still with us and the struggles of Moses and others are still a reality. But so too is the God who continues to liberate people.

To the preacher. Jesus' observation that 'a prophet is without honour in his own country' may be true, but the preacher is still called to be a prophet.

Renewal

Text: Christ rules there above all heavenly rulers, authorities, powers and lords; he has a title superior to all titles of authority in this world and in the next. God put all things under Christ's feet and gave him to the church as supreme Lord over all things. **(Ephesians 1.21-22, GNB)**

Sermon notes by
Jember Teferra

AIM

To help people, as the Millennium dawns, to uphold the Lordship and supremacy of Christ, who alone can make the world a better place to live in.

based on readings for
Week 6
(February 6 – 12,
2000)

Introduction

Advanced in technology, science and other secular inventions, the world today is materially comfortable. It is also a mess. Improved information technology brings us 'doom and gloom', war, man-made and natural disasters, lack of justice and equity, immorality, materialism, crime and so on. What can Christians aim to do about it?

'Jesus Christ is Lord'

● **Uphold the Lordship of our Lord.** Only leaders with Christian values, who acknowledge, uncompromisingly, the authority of Jesus and uphold the values he promotes, will make the world a better place to live in. Upholding the Lordship of Jesus could deal with the root causes of problems related to materialism and morality, and eliminate racism, oppression and abuse of human rights at all levels and in all circumstances.

● **Uphold the values of our Lord.** Only the values taught by Jesus on issues of social justice can bring about equity, good governance and no abuse of power, whatever positions Christian leaders may hold.

Conclusion Such change is not humanly possible. Only the Holy Spirit can prepare us to bring about God's Kingdom on earth in the year 2000 by upholding the absolute authority and Lordship of Jesus Christ instead of predicting 'doom and gloom', and by refusing to listen to false prophecy.

To the preacher. How do we promote the absolute authority and Lordship of our Lord in practical terms? Do you present Jesus as a role model at all levels of leadership? Please discuss this with your congregation.

You are called

Sermon notes by
Tom Arthur

based on readings for
Week 7
(February 13 – 19,
2000)

'Turning the world upside down'

Text: Naaman, commander of the army of the king of Aram, was a great man and in high favour with his master, because by him the Lord had given victory to Aram. The man, though a mighty warrior, suffered from leprosy. (2 Kings 5.1, NRSV)

AIM
To encourage people to be used as channels for God's healing power.

Introduction
This story reverses our expectations of the way the world works in order to teach an important lesson about vocation: our calling to ministry (which includes all Christians who take discipleship seriously) is not to prove our own strength and abilities, but to become open channels for God working through us.

● **Feeling overwhelmed.** Confronted with the task of healing Naaman, the kings of Aram and Israel feel overwhelmed. In what ways do the congregation feel overwhelmed by impossible tasks, or threatened in their efforts to be a faithful community by the expectations and values of the world? Where do we feel most powerless?

● **Feeling powerless.** Ordinary means of problem solving fail. Note how the story is told. Everything — power, honour, conquest — is turned upside down. The great army commander, Naaman, has leprosy. The king of Aram is instructed by a captive Israelite girl, and reduced to sending tribute to the king of Israel whose lands he has been raiding. The king of Israel, feeling powerless, says, 'Am I God?' All traditional means of control fail in the face of Naaman's leprosy. Where in today's world do we see traditional means of power and control failing to manage situations that call for healing?

● **The solution.** Only the prophet Elisha can solve Naaman's problem. He does this simply by pointing to the sacred history of a people who have been guided by God into a way of life governed by Law (Torah), responsibility and respect rather than power and conquest, privilege and arrogance. The symbolic character of the miracle is important: Elisha sends Naaman to the River Jordan, where God's people entered the promised land and renewed the covenant *(Joshua 24)*. What heals is a new way of life that turns the world upside down. How can we, in our vocation, step out of the spotlight, leave behind the traditional ways of authority, and point the way to a relationship with God?

To the preacher. You should be able to find plenty of examples from world news of worldly authority and power failing where healing is needed.

You are forgiven

Text: 'I, I am He who blots out your transgressions for my own sake, and I will not remember your sins.'
(Isaiah 43.25, RSV)

Sermon notes by
Lloyda Fanusie

*based on readings for
Week 8
(February 20 – 26,
2000)*

AIM
To remind Christians that God's unconditional love affirms our forgiveness.

Introduction
We often take the word 'forgiveness' for granted — we all ask for it. How do we know that God forgives? It is a matter of faith: our faith in God's goodness and God's faith in a renewed and cleansed 'returned sinner'. The prophets have often spoken about God's saving acts; as Christians we believe in Christ's salvation.

● **The human desire for power makes it hard to say no to**

'God's magnanimity'

the forces of evil. What can help us? Conscience, the Id and Ego of psychology, your cultural norms.

● **Refer to a few stories about forgiveness** (both personal and biblical).

● **Being aware of our broken human condition is faith's first step towards transformation**. This awareness comes through the influence of others, norms and standards, and sometimes from an inner struggle to rise above evil. Our spirituality enables us to acknowledge that God is on our side.

● **God's magnanimity towards our frailties is a way of healing and saving us physically and spiritually.** This takes us further in our journey of faith as we become new people. Repentance is essential to our spiritual growth — God loves us in spite of everything.

Conclusion Once we have reached a deep inner strength as renewed people, we shall want to spread the good news to others. They too are enfolded in God's love and we are all safe in God's hands. This means that no principalities and powers have any power over us.

To the preacher. Remind people that forgiveness is a gift of God, and stress the great feelings of relief and release which come from being forgiven. Encourage people to appreciate the virtues of faith, hope and love.

You are loved

Sermon notes by
Elina Templin

based on the readings for
Week 9
(February 27 – March 4, 2000)

Text: 'I will betroth you to me for ever ... in righteousness and justice, in love and compassion ... and you will acknowledge the Lord.'
(Hosea 2.19-20, NIV)

AIM
To encourage people to trust that in Christ we are connected to God forever.

● **A disconnected people.** Some people feel that the greatest pain of our time is disconnectedness. Everywhere, age-old ties and ways are being threatened, broken down, with nothing substantial to replace them. But God promises to bind his own together in a love that can never be broken.

● **An undeserving people.** The tragedy of Christian vows of betrothal in marriage, which sooner or later lead to separation, divorce, or unfaithfulness, seems to make a mockery of today's text. We are indeed a 'sin-sick' people — a good old evangelical term, outdated perhaps, but the gospel truth! We can't get life right. We need a doctor to heal our brokenness. It is God who speaks these words to us, and God never breaks his word.

● **A loved people.** Thus our salvation can never depend on what we do, but on what God has done for us in Jesus on the cross. So we can relax! We do not always have to keep proving ourselves. We are loved! We are a letter sent by God to others, speaking and living out his righteousness, justice, love and compassion. As a minister in Johannesburg, I would sometimes wear my clerical collar when driving. Without it, I freely indulged in impatient, angry gestures or looks; wearing it, such actions were unthinkable! It reminded me that I am a child of God and need to behave as such.

Conclusion Are you living as a letter from God, wearing an invisible collar as God's minister? How are you bringing the redemptive healing love of God to others? How can you most effectively be a letter from God to others (including your enemy) in your personal context?

To the preacher. What is preventing you from being a more loving example of the Good News of God's grace and compassion?

You are changed

Sermon notes by
Isaiah Gaddala

based on readings for
Week 10
(March 5 – 11, 2000)

*'An outward
expression of
an inward
change'*

Text: Produce fruit in keeping with repentance.
(Luke 3.8, NIV)

AIM
To help the congregation understand that God expects them to show their changed life.

Introduction
Remind your congregation of the origins of Ash Wednesday. We live in an age which expects much — but without any sacrifice. The craze for slimming is to look more attractive physically. Sadly, many Christians also try to put on a show in Lent in order to look more 'spiritual'.

● **True religion does not consist only in outward acts.** Being religious is more than doing religious actions! Our church attendance, hymn singing, almsgiving, prayers, fasting and the like do not automatically make us Christians. Other religious people also do these 'acts' — even more! Behind them can be a desire to buy our entry into heaven. Religion becomes a commodity that is available and freely accessible, and God is seen as someone who is at our 'beck and call'. We do certain things to earn his favour.

● **True religion is an outward expression of an inward change, not a matter of mere external acts.** An evil heart cannot produce good deeds. Before God accepts our religious activities there has to be an act of repentance on our part, a change of mind from relying on self to turning to God. Mental change precedes acts of piety. When the self is oriented towards God our religion becomes authentic.

● **God's call today is to be authentic (real), not simply religious.** Authentic Christian life is a life of discipleship, a costly following of the one who said, 'If anyone would come after me, he must deny himself and take up his cross daily and follow me' *(Luke 9.23)*. This is not a call to deny a few things (as many people do during Lent) but the denial of self itself. The selfish self has to die before the true self is born! And this new birth brings a new perspective on the whole of life. Life is truly related — to God in utter dependence, to self in honest opinion, and to others through deeds of mercy and faithfulness. This is true religion *(James 1.26, 27)*.

To the preacher. Do not discourage people from doing religious activities, but help them to know the real meaning of religion. Encourage repentance, renewal and radical discipleship.

Light, love and darkness 1

Text: 'You should not be surprised at my saying, "You must be born again." The wind blows wherever it pleases. You hear its sound, but you cannot tell where it comes from or where it is going. So it is with everyone born of the Spirit.' **(John 3.7 – 8, NIV)**

Sermon notes by
Elina Templin

based on readings for
Week 11
(March 12 – 18,
2000)

AIM
To remind people that when God is at the centre of our lives, we are all born-again Christians.

'Believing is seeing'

Introduction
Conflict is a constant thread running through the Gospel of John: conflict between Jesus and those who judge by human standards; conflict with those whose prejudice blinds them to his identity; and Jesus' efforts as he tries to pierce the darkness of their resistance; all this is present almost from the very beginning of the Gospel.

● **Seeing is believing.** Our modern world conditions us to trust in what we see as the only truth. But Jesus attacks this thinking. We only truly see, he says, when we trust. We will only truly understand the things of God through a living faith, and when we obey and act on what we believe.

● **Believing is seeing.** So the Christian way is understanding in and through faith. Turn — and trust.

The heart of the Christian life is so simple that even a child can do it. Indeed, only a childlike faith — fresh, open, trusting, unprejudiced — will guide us into the quality of life which Jesus promises us.

Conclusion Lent is a time for looking deeper. How much do I desire the things of God, God himself? How much am I dying in order to be born again?

To the preacher. Share with your congregation (or they could share with you?) times when you have experienced the light of Christ breaking through or breaking down personal, social or religious prejudice.

Light, love and darkness 2

Sermon notes by
Elina Templin

based on readings for
Week 12
(March 19 – 25, 2000)

'Hold to the Word'

Text: 'If you hold to my teaching, you are really my disciples. Then you will know the truth, and the truth will set you free.'   (John 8.31 – 32, NIV)

AIM
To help people see that the way to resist darkness and live in the light of God's love is to hold to his Word.

● **Hooked into sin.** Where can we find a more profound picture of being 'hooked' into the slavery of sin than in Genesis 3? 'Did God really say...?' It seems so reasonable, so harmless... But appearances can deceive. The great deceiver, the devil, is the father of lies, and 'does not hold to the truth' *(verse 44)*. When we are in Satan's grip, we cannot see the light, or desire it.

● **Holding to the truth.** Jesus' greatest criticism is aimed at the hypocrisy of the Pharisees. Something, or someone, is not as it seems. There is a lack of unity between the outer and inner being, a break, a lack of integrity. But Jesus promises that when we hold to his teaching, and allow God's Word to shape and influence us, we become his disciples and our life takes on a new dimension of wholeness.

Conclusion Therefore, hold fast, stand fast, stick close to me, says Jesus, because the journey is long and the way is narrow. But your reward, even now, will be great, for you will recognize God in Christ and become free to be a child of God.

To the preacher. Picture the movement of Lent as a time when God will shape you and your congregation, for example as a potter shapes his clay; you may be able to use this idea as a visual aid in some imaginative way.

Rejection and hope 1

Text: **Therefore many of the Jews who had come to visit Mary, and had seen what Jesus did, put their faith in him. But some of them went to the Pharisees and told them what Jesus had done.**
(John 11.45 – 46, NIV)

Sermon notes by
Ngozi Okeke

based on readings for
Week 13
(March 26 – April
1, 2000)

AIM
To encourage people to learn through the example of Jesus and put opposition or rejection in perspective.

Introduction
Look at the different responses to the raising of Lazarus. Some believed; others became spies for the religious leaders; the religious leaders plotted Jesus' downfall. When God is at work, not everyone will welcome it.

'Not
everyone
objects!'

● Why do people oppose the work of God?

- **Lack of spiritual insight.** Ignorance very often breeds insecurity and irrational behaviour.

- **Being set in their ways** and preferring to remain within their comfort zone. To risk venturing out of that comfort zone to embrace the new things God is doing means an uncertain future — a sacrifice some people are not prepared to make.

- **The need to be in control,** like the Jewish leaders. Following the unpredictable Holy Spirit means living on the edge — not a place where control freaks feel comfortable.

● How can Jesus' response inform our own attitude?

- **Jesus was right but he chose not to press the point.** When we are unjustly attacked, we often want to defend ourselves and stand our ground. Why? Is it always necessary? Like Jesus we need to know how to choose his battles.

- **Jesus did not court controversy unnecessarily.** He withdrew from public life to give both himself and his attackers a breathing space. A cooling off period is always a good idea!

- **Jesus made the best of the situation and did what he could sensibly do** — he taught his disciples in private.

Conclusion Opposition to the work of God may signal a change of direction, not an end. We need to ask the Spirit for discernment so that, like Jesus and Paul, we can know when to stay and fight God's corner and when to move on to new, divinely appointed, pastures. The most important thing is to be in tune with God so that we can hear what he is saying in each situation.

To the preacher. Have you engaged in any unnecessary battles lately? How do you balance the desire to avoid controversy with the need to provide strong leadership?

Rejection and hope 2

Sermon notes by
Ngozi Okeke

based on readings for
Week 14
(April 2 – 8, 2000)

Text: 'In My Father's house are many rooms ... I am going there to prepare a place for you. And ... I will come back and take you to be with me that you also may be where I am.' (John 14.2 – 3, NIV)

AIM
To encourage us to face our trials with hope.

Introduction
Owning a house in underdeveloped countries usually means starting from scratch — buying the land, employing an architect and then contracting a builder. In

the West, most people simply secure a mortgage and buy a house — or, if they live in a major tourist attraction like a palace or stately home, they may inherit it. Jesus offers us mansions above. How do we qualify?

● **By inheritance.** To inherit, we have to be born into the family or have it bequeathed to us by the owner at his or her death. The same goes for our heavenly mansions. We can inherit it only through spiritual birth into God's family *(John 3.3)*.

● **By building.** Building a mansion takes time, effort and money, but the resulting beauty is worth the expense. Jesus puts time and effort into preparing our eternal dwelling, because he thinks we are worth it.

● **By preparation.** Preparing the person who inherits the palace also takes time — from birth until they inherit! The heirs may not always like their training by parents or teachers, but accept it as unavoidable. The same is true of us. Jesus puts great effort into preparing us to inherit a mansion, and made sure before he left that our preparation would be continued by the Holy Spirit, our Counsellor and Helper. We may not always like it, but God uses all our different situations to mould us into the image of his Son.

Conclusion Jesus comforts his troubled disciples with the promise of a glorious eternal reunion with him, which he will be busy preparing. Trials and temptations are inconveniences on the way. This should offer encouragement and hope. Like the disciples, we do not always understand, but like them we have a clear promise and a hope which Jesus intended would keep them, and us after them, pressing forward.

To the preacher. Do you encourage people to look forward in hope to the eternal mansions? And take comfort from it when you struggle with the demands of your ministry?

The way of the cross 1

Sermon notes by
Estela Lamas

based on readings for
Week 15
(April 9 – 15, 2000)

'Be free to serve'

Text: 'I am the true vine, and my Father is the vinedresser. Every branch of mine that bears no fruit, he takes away, and every branch that does bear fruit he prunes, that it may bear more fruit.'

(John 15.1 – 2, RSV)

AIM
To encourage sharing in Jesus' life, by freely choosing to serve him.

Introduction
How did the disciples feel, listening to Jesus' farewell discourse in the isolation of the Upper Room? Invite your hearers to join them there, feeling the presence and love of Jesus and listening to what he says.

● **Learning from Jesus.** When we share in Jesus' life, we can feel his presence in our lives, walk with him every day and learn about him. However, more important than learning *about* him is to learn *from* him, listening to his teaching, observing his ways and actions and accepting him as a model.

● **Choosing to serve.** Experiencing God's love through Jesus, being united in Christ, makes it possible for us to choose to love our fellow men and women and serve them as Jesus chose to love and serve us. Our experience of God's love for us 'forces' us, by an inner and deep feeling of identification, to serve our neighbour.

● **Witnessing to God's love.** God, in his great and deep love, offered us his son's sinless life as a gift. Witnessing to God's love is the way to help the world community to become a Christian community; it creates the necessary conditions to overcome injustice and make a place for justice and peace.

Conclusion We must be grateful for God's gift and rejoice in the resurrection, which makes it possible for us to extend the Christian community and offer eternal life to all.

To the preacher. How can you encourage your congregation to engage in mission? Explore with them ways of serving the community, following Jesus' example on his way to the cross.

The way of the cross 2

Text: 'As you sent me into the world, I have sent them into the world.' (John 17.18, NIV)

Sermon notes by
Peter Tongeman

based on readings for
Week 16
(April 16 – 22,
2000)

AIM
To show, from Jesus' prayer, his expectations for his followers.

'Sent into
the world'

Introduction
Jesus knew he was drawing near to the end of life. His trial and crucifixion were imminent. It was almost time to hand over to his disciples responsibility for spreading the gospel message. In prayer he commended them to his Father. What he asked for them applies to all who follow Jesus today.

● **Holy.** They were to be holy people *(verse 17)*: set apart for God's use, reflecting the character of Jesus himself. 'Without holiness no one will see the Lord' *(Hebrews 12.14)*. This will not be achieved by withdrawing from the life of the world *(verse 15)*, but rather by adopting kingdom life-style and values in the midst of the world.

● **Sent.** They were commissioned by Jesus to be his agents in a troubled world *(verse 18)*. Led by them, the Church was born and grew until there were Christian communities throughout the world. Today's disciples are also under orders, sent out to continue Jesus' mission *(Matthew 28.19 – 20)*.

● **Equipped.** Jesus, in his teaching, gave his disciples words of truth *(verse 14)*. With these they were equipped to bring the light of understanding to others. He also gave them a spirit of infectious joy *(verse 13)*, so that

Christianity was caught as well as taught.

● **United.** Unity of purpose, harmony of relationships, inclusive love *(verses 21, 23)*. These became the hallmarks of true discipleship. They were to be one with each other as Jesus is one with the Father, showing a divided world a better way.

Conclusion When Jesus prayed for his followers, he included us *(verse 20)*. We too have been sent into the world as his representatives, to demonstrate kingdom living by word and action.

To the preacher. Examine your own life. Is it characterized by holiness, joy, harmony? Do others recognize you as one 'sent' by Jesus?

The victory of love

Sermon notes by
Rodney Dreyer

based on readings for
Week 17
(April 23 – 29, 2000)

'Jesus our hope'

Text: Then they told what had happened on the road.
(Luke 24.35, NRSV)

AIM
To realize afresh that Jesus is our heart's hope as we travel through life.

Introduction
Many things happen to people on the roads of our world. We meet many different people and strangers. On the road children are born, people die. On the road new insights are discovered, hopes and fears are realized. When we travel along roads, on land and in our life, our minds are filled with many thoughts — what we have said and done, people we have left behind, what the future holds.

● **Two travellers.** In the Gospel two men are on the road to Emmaus. They are downcast. They had 'hoped', but now their hope has died. There is no future for them now. Jesus their leader is dead.

● **The stranger.** But the risen Jesus, a stranger to them, joins them on the road. He asks them a question to find out exactly where they are. They are amazed. What a question! They are surprised and share their surprise with him. He speaks to them and hope begins to rise in their hearts. He explains the Scriptures to them and they understand as never before.

● **Recognition.** They leave the road as they reach their homes. They invite him to stay with them. He breaks bread with them. They recognize him in this. Hope is restored to their hearts which burned as he talked to them on the road.

Conclusion We too on the road of our life are often depressed, downcast and disillusioned. We have little hope, there is no future for us. Our lives provide no answers to the deep questions we have. Who will give us back this hope? The same Jesus who gave back hope to those two disciples. But he does not impose himself on us. He waits to be invited.

To the preacher. Become aware of the importance of the Word and the Sacrament in our common worship. Examine ways in which the 'Word has become flesh' for you on life's roads and crossroads.

Community of love

Text: Dear children, let us not love with words or tongue but with actions and in truth.   (1 John 3.18, NIV)

Sermon notes by
Joy Pegg

based on readings for
Week 18
(April 30 – May 6,
2000)

AIM
To consider how we can begin to love someone we do not 'love'.

'Love in action'

Introduction
We want to be obedient and love this person, but somehow they just get under our skin. What are we to do? We cry, 'Don't tell me; show me!' God, who is love, has sent his Son to show us what love is like in action.

● **The Golden Rule.** How would we act if we did love them? Luke *(Luke 6.31)* describes Jesus referring to this in the context of loving those you do not like. He gives general guidelines first *(Luke 6.27-28)*, and then the examples become more specific *(Luke 6.29-30)*. But we need to take care. The principles are general (kindness, respect, etc.) but the particulars need to be more specific. See how Jesus met each person as an individual.

● **Just do it.** It may be that, to begin with, loving this particular person is a matter of sheer obedience. Consider the struggle Jesus had in the Garden. John gives Jesus as our supreme example *(1 John 3.16)*. He struggled but he did it.

● **Rejoice in the change.** As you obey, you will grow, and bear the fruit of the Spirit: love, joy, peace... *(Galatians 5.22)*. Very soon you will find that loving that person is not the burden it had been, and you will be loving in truth.

Conclusion God is love and the writer to the Hebrews tells us that 'in the past God spoke [words] ... but in these last days he has spoken to us by his Son [action and example]' *(Hebrews 1.1 – 2)*. And since Jesus is 'the exact representation of his [God's] being' *(Hebrews 1.3)*, we can really know what love in action is like.

To the preacher. What other examples of Jesus' love in action can you think of? Can you share a time when you loved someone you did not like?

People of faith

Text: You must make every effort to support your faith with goodness, and goodness with knowledge, and knowledge with self-control, and self-control with endurance, and endurance with godliness, and godliness with mutual affection, and mutual affection with love. (2 Peter 1.5 – 7, NRSV)

Sermon notes by
Catherine Middleton

AIM
To encourage worshippers to be a creative and supportive Christian community.

based on readings for
Week 19
(May 7 – 13, 2000)

'Mutual encouragement'

● **Supporting.** The church community is described as a group of people who are supporting each other in trying to live by the values of the gospel. Give some examples of these values, based on the ideals listed in the text.

● **Living by values.** The writer of 2 Peter recognizes that part of the difficulty of living by these values is that the world beyond the Church lives by quite different values, and Christians are not impervious to them. Draw some parallels between the world of the first Christians and the world you and your hearers inhabit.

● **Helping.** Each Christian is called to help other Christians in their efforts to live by gospel values rather than secular ones. Draw attention to some examples where this is already happening. Gently suggest areas where more help could be given.

● **Relying.** Many will find this encouragement to take part in the Church's ministry daunting. In verses 3 and 4 the writer assures readers that, in Christ, we have been given 'everything needed for life and godliness'. No special gifts and graces are needed for this ministry. We have them already. But we do need to learn to rely on them and use them more bravely and effectively.

Conclusion Let us commit ourselves to living in such a way that the Church is continually becoming a more loving and open community, bearing witness to the resurrection through the way we live our life together.

To the preacher. Compare the life of a church or denomination you know well with the pattern set out in this passage. Where have 'secular' values become so ingrained in the life of the Church that they hinder it from living by gospel values?

Encounter with Judaism 1

Sermon notes by
Peter Cotterell

based on readings for
Week 20
(May 14 – 20, 2000)

'A covenant people'

Text: You prepare a table before me in the presence of my enemies. You anoint my head with oil; my cup overflows. **(Psalm 23.5, NIV)**

AIM
To explore Psalm 23 as a Covenant Psalm and recognize its relevance for Christians as the people of the New Covenant.

Introduction
This is one the best-known and best-loved psalms. It has given hope, courage, comfort and strength to many generations of believers. The image of God as a caring Good Shepherd strikes an immediate chord with many people. Here is One who is actively involved in the lives of his people, who provides for us, leading us into good places. Here is One whom we can trust and whose protection is experienced even in the darkest valleys of our lives. Sheep from many different countries and cultures have come to know this Shepherd.

● **From shepherd to king.** Note that in verse 5 there is a change of image which is not always appreciated. The shepherd and his sheep give way to a king entering into a covenant relationship. Explain the significance of a feast as a part of the covenant process and the joy of David, whose enemies can only look on, powerless to intervene.

● **A covenant of grace.** The covenant celebrated in Psalm 23 is a covenant of grace. Explore what is meant by a covenant of grace, in which God is the active party and his people the recipients of his favour.

● **The new covenant in Christ.** Explore the new covenant in Christ established through the cross. Celebrate the wonder of God's love: we are both the sheep of his pasture and the beneficiaries of a new covenant. As we pass through a valley of the shadow of death, and even in the presence of enemies, God is present to bless.

Conclusion Offer a prayer of thanksgiving for God's wonderful love and the amazing nature of his new covenant in Christ.

To the preacher. Reflect on your own relationship with Jesus. Does it reflect the reality of the new covenant of grace into which you have been baptized?

Encounter with Judaism 2

Text: My God, my God, why have you forsaken me? Why are you so far from saving me, so far from the words of my groaning? (Psalm 22.1, NIV)

Sermon notes by
Elina Templin

AIM
To show that wholehearted prayer is the only way to a real relationship with God.

based on readings for
Week 21
(May 21 – 27, 2000)

'A living faith'

Introduction
For thousands of years, the Psalms have reflected the human condition and touched a universal chord beyond all religious boundaries. At some time or another, all Christians, like the Psalmist, experience God as absent. Here is God, absent, silent and seemingly uncaring. But we see that it is precisely in times of testing that the Psalmist's faith is most alive. Why is it so real?

● **He is honest.** How often people say, 'But I can't say that to God when I pray!' How often do we keep our boredom, doubts and complaints away from God? But the Psalmist does not hesitate to accuse God of forsaking him, and groaning about what is happening to him.

● **He remembers.** The Psalmist pours out his heart and

soul to God and gives his life completely over to God. There is room now for him to remember what God has done, how God has been his help and refuge in the past. God remains God — the Most High, the Holy One, the Lord. Suffering, sin and death will never have the last word.

● **He praises.** He begins with lament and complaint but, as he remembers, is lifted up to praise, and able to look at the bigger picture. 'All the ends of the earth will remember' *(verse 27)*.

Conclusion An encounter with the living God becomes real when we bring our whole being to God — trusting in faith that he is near, in spite of how we feel. Does praying make a difference in your life? How? If not, why not?

To the preacher. What areas of your life remain closed off to the probing light of Christ?

Encounter with other faiths 1

Sermon notes by
Isaiah Gaddala

based on readings for
Week 22
(May 28 – June 3, 2000)

'Follow the promptings of the Spirit'

Text: **Always be prepared to give an answer to everyone who asks you to give the reason for the hope that you have.** **(1 Peter 3.15b, NIV)**

AIM
To encourage the congregation to interact meaningfully with people of other faiths.

Introduction
Set the tone for worship by sharing an encounter with people of other faiths, from your own experience if possible. The attitude you adopt will influence your congregation. Today, instead of going to other parts of the world to serve as missionaries, the mission fields have moved into our neighbourhood.

● **Be led by the Spirit.** In reaching out to the unreached, be led by the Spirit rather than being moved by statistics. Obeying the call of God is more important than 'plunging' into mission work to tackle the need around you. Peter had to obey the vision that God gave him to carry the gospel to the Gentiles. Although he had seen the conversion of the Gentile Samaritans *(Acts 8)*, it took the 'nudge' of the Spirit in the form of a repeated vision to make him cross the racial boundaries.

● **Do not hesitate.** Once the Spirit guides, there should be no hesitation or barriers placed in the way of carrying out the call of God. Obedience is not complete if it is prefaced with a 'but'. If Jesus is Lord, he must be obeyed totally and unconditionally. The Lord had to 'convert' Peter (from his racial and ethnic prejudices) before sending him to the household of the Gentile Cornelius to share the gospel with them. Be prepared for the 'surprises' God may send when he makes us his messengers.

● **Be clear.** In presenting the gospel to a 'gentile' audience, it is important to share clearly the 'core' gospel: the earthly life and ministry, death and resurrection of Jesus — Jesus as Messiah, Saviour and Judge. But also share the blessings of the gospel; the coming of the Holy Spirit; incorporation into the Church of God through baptism; and the need for continual nurture in the newfound faith.

To the preacher. Remind your congregation about the great commission given in Matthew 28.18 – 20, which includes the 'discipling' of all the 'nations' till he comes, and, following the agenda of Acts 1.8, begin at your 'Jerusalem' but go out to the ends of the earth.

Encounter with other faiths 2

Sermon notes by
Supriyo Mukherjee

based on readings for
Week 23
(June 4 – 10, 2000)

'God so loved the world'

Text: 'When the bow is in the clouds, I will see it and remembcr the everlasting covenant between God and every living creature of all flesh that is on the earth.' **(Genesis 9.16, NRSV)**

AIM

To remind people that God's love is given freely to all people.

● **God makes his covenant with his creation.** In the Old Testament, water is regarded as chaos — God created the world by removing the water from the earth *(Genesis 1)*. In the New Testament, water is the water of baptism. In Noah's story, God makes a covenant with his creation that the water of chaos will never destroy it; the whole world is thus baptized, foreshadowing the New Covenant established in Jesus: 'For God so loved the world that he gave his only Son' *(John 3.16)*.

● **Noah's Ark and the cross of Jesus.** Like Noah gathering one pair of all living creatures into the Ark to save them from death, Jesus also saves all humanity from the curse of death. The obedience of Jesus cancels the condemnation inherited as a result of the disobedience of Adam *(Romans 5.12 – 21)*. Jesus does not condemn anyone except the self-righteous and he commands us not to judge or condemn *(Luke 6.37)*.

Conclusion Gospel means Good News, not the bad news of condemnation. If we proclaim the Good News of God's love for the world, then the world will receive salvation.

To the preacher. Contrast the attitude of Jesus, rebuking the violence of his disciples *(Luke 9.51 – 56)* with the attitude of people in the Old Testament towards, e.g., the prophets of Baal *(1 Kings 18)*.

Making us one

Text: All of them were filled with the Holy Spirit.
(Acts 2.4, NIV)

Sermon notes by
Rodney Dreyer

based on readings for
Week 24
(June 11 – 17, 2000)

AIM
To reassure ourselves that the Spirit comes repeatedly to renew our lives.

'Given to each person'

Introduction
Everyone is aware of the awesome power of the wind. Hurricanes and tornados bend and break trees. For some, these winds are the beginning of the wet season, the coming of the rains. So wind can fill us with fear, but also bring new life.

● **The Pentecost wind.** In the story of Pentecost we read of another powerful wind that filled a house. The disciples of Jesus were alone and afraid. Jesus had been crucified, was risen and had promised that something, someone would come to them. Then 'they will be filled with the Holy Spirit'.

● **Given to each person.** Something great, strange and marvellous possessed them. God's Spirit came into them, and they were never the same again. Their hearts were changed, fear gave way to courage. But we must remember that the Spirit is given to each person. Each of us is purified, cleansed and strengthened, lit up by a fire which burns within us.

● **The breath of life.** God breathed the breath of life into us in our mother's womb. At our baptism God breathed into us his very own life, so that his Holy Spirit is now in us and we are in him. And this same life of God's Spirit is later confirmed and strengthens us, so that we begin to grow in a new way.

Conclusion Each year, when we remember the coming of the Holy Spirit at Pentecost, God breathes his Spirit into us again, to make us new again. The fruit of the Spirit begins to grow in us. As no farmer would say, 'I do not need the rains this year, I can cope on my own', so we would be foolish to say, 'I do not need the Holy Spirit, I can cope on my own'. Instead, let us ask God to renew the earth and his Church, transform our lives, train our hearts and teach us his truth by sending his Holy Spirit.

To the preacher. How does the Spirit transform your life? What in your life needs to be bent and broken by the wind of the Spirit?

Sending us to each other

Sermon notes by
Valerie Ogden

based on readings for
Week 25
(June 18 – 24, 2000)

'Raise up teachers'

Text: **When [Barnabas] found [Saul], he took him to Antioch, and for a whole year the two met with the people of the church and taught a large group.** (Acts 11.26, GNB)

AIM
To affirm teaching as a ministry of the Church.

Introduction
Most people can recall particular teachers to whom they are grateful and certain lessons that have stuck with them for life. (Find personal examples.) Here, Saul and Barnabas are shown exercising a lengthy, committed teaching ministry to one group of believers. What can we learn from this for today's Church?

● **Teach to build.** There were many Gentile converts in Antioch and news about them had spread to Jerusalem. Barnabas was sent to oversee the situation, but first he praised the Antioch church and rejoiced with them. A good teacher always builds on what he or she finds. Not, 'Is this all you've done?' But rather, 'Haven't you done well so far!'

● **Teach together.** Barnabas didn't begin the teaching programme in the Antioch church alone. He went to find a more experienced teacher, Saul, and they worked together. How often in our churches do teachers 'go it alone' rather than drawing on others? (Explore team teaching as a tool for mission: different teachers are blessed with different gifts and graces, so let us use them.)

● **Teach consistently.** Paul and Barnabas spent a full year teaching the Antioch church, yet for some in our congregations, one evening's Bible study is too demanding! (Explore reasons for this in your own context without being simplistic or judgemental.) Teaching courses such as *Disciple* and *Alpha,* popular in the UK, affirm that consistent, quality teaching over a long period can produce results. (Use local examples.)

Conclusion A teaching ministry will restore confidence in ourselves as a Church, so we need to encourage teachers to do the work.

To the preacher. Make the point, if appropriate, that not all are called to a teaching ministry — this may challenge some to recognize their need to be pupils. This sermon may be particularly useful before beginning a teaching series for your church.

Giving life

Text: **And [Jesus] awoke and rebuked the wind, and said to the sea, 'Peace! Be still!' And the wind ceased, and there was a great calm.**

(Mark 4.39, RSV)

Sermon notes by
Philip Wadham

based on readings for
Week 26
(June 25 – July 1,
2000)

AIM
To recognize that God's Spirit is experienced in different ways.

Introduction
The Hebrew word for Spirit is 'ru-ach' which is also the word for 'wind'. The beginning of creation can be read as 'the wind of God was moving over the face of the waters' *(Genesis 1.2b)*. Creation wind can be experienced as a refreshing, gentle breeze or a storm-force gale. Which of these two do we associate with God's Spirit?

'One Spirit, various moods'

● **Powerful.** When the disciples and others set out to cross the sea it was presumably calm. Without warning the 'great storm of wind' developed and was threatening, even to experienced sailors. All, except Jesus, were afraid for their lives. Do we ever experience God's Spirit as powerful and frightening, something that we, though experienced Christians, can't quite handle? (Invite comments from your listeners. Connect this story to Pentecost, also a frightening experience initially.)

● **Peaceful.** Whilst the storm raged Jesus slept. How could he? Exhaustion? Perhaps, but Mark may have another intention. (Ask for suggestions, or give some yourself: the sleep of a just person, a strong faith, etc.) Jesus responds to their fear by acting to calm it. He commands, 'Peace. Be still', and 'there was a great calm'. (Give and ask for examples of when God's peace has transformed turmoil to calm.)

Conclusion Very often people associate God's Spirit with peace and calm, saying things like, 'I love to go to church and experience God's presence in its peace and quiet.' That is indeed true, and an important aspect of the Spirit, but the Spirit is also a powerful force for change, both personal and corporate. That in itself can be a frightening prospect.

To the preacher. Involving your listeners in a dialogue, if you can, rather than just preaching at them, can be a very rewarding experience. But that too is a frightening thing to do!

After war and exile... 1

Text: 'You see the trouble we are in: Jerusalem lies in ruins, and its gates have been burned with fire. Come, let us rebuild the wall of Jerusalem, and we will no longer be in disgrace.'
(Nehemiah 2.17 – 18, NIV)

Sermon notes by
Joy Pegg

AIM
To suggest a way forward when all is confusion, pain, and destruction.

based on readings for
Week 27
(July 2 – 8, 2000)

'Re-establish the boundaries'

Introduction
At some point in our lives most of us will experience 'war', 'destruction' or 'disintegration' of some kind. The thought of rebuilding seems overwhelming. But if the process can be broken down into smaller steps, a way forward can be found. There are principles we can follow from Nehemiah's experience.

● **Feel the pain.** There must be a period of mourning. Denial of the devastation that has been caused and the pain that is being experienced will only impede recovery. Be totally open before God and then allow him to pour in his healing balm.

● **Assess the damage.** Nehemiah could have been distracted from his main goal by the amount of damage he could see all around him as he travelled down through Israel. But he had singled out Jerusalem as the key area for restoration. We also need to identify the key area in our own situations.

● **Repair the breach.** Jerusalem needed its defining and protective walls to be rebuilt. What can we build on that is still remaining? As well as protection, access was provided via the gates. We must beware of blocking everything out, or building a wall that is so strong we will never be hurt again. We should work with the part that is nearest to hand and not be afraid to let others do their part in helping.

Conclusion We can't do everything at once. We must establish the key area, define that part and repair it.

To the preacher. Reflect on your own experience of 'war' and the way that you attempted to rebuild after destruction.

After war and exile... 2

Sermon notes by
Joy Pegg

based on readings for
Week 28
(July 9 – 15, 2000)

'Renew the community'

Text: All the people assembled as one man ... They told Ezra the scribe to bring out the Book of the Law of Moses. (Nehemiah 8.1, NIV)

AIM
To promote wholeness in a community or individual after tragedy.

Introduction
After a communal tragedy there is the danger of fragmenting into disparate groups, each one engulfed in its own misery. It often requires someone from outside the immediate problem to restore a common focus. This can even happen with an individual. How can we facilitate healing?

● **Get exposed to the word of God.** In the darkness and emptiness at the beginning God spoke his creative word: '...and it was so' *(Genesis 1)*. He is always a God who speaks. It will be in different ways for each one, but we need to hear that sure word for ourselves. In Nehemiah's time the Jews needed help in understanding the language because they had forgotten it. We might need help as well.

● **Exchange sorrow for the joy of the Lord.** There comes a point when we need to turn away from the pain, anguish, regrets and anger. Sometimes we need help to realize this. Although the people of Jerusalem still had things that needed sorting out, they were encouraged to rejoice at that point. The joy of the Lord (not their own worked-up emotion) would be their strength.

● **Obey the word in practice.** It is often cathartic to actually get up and do something. All around the Jews were houses lying in ruins, and building temporary booths or shelters may have seemed irrelevant. But they obeyed in this and the more permanent work followed later.

Conclusion Rebuilding takes time and it is essential to give yourself time. Renewal is not a 'quick fix' procedure, but rather a process.

To the preacher. In what circumstances have you discovered that 'the joy of the Lord' was your strength? Could you share this?

People with disabilities

Text: When Jesus saw her, he called her forward and said to her, 'Woman, you are set free from your infirmity.' Then he put his hands on her, and immediately she straightened up and praised God. **(Luke 13.12 – 13, NIV)**

Sermon notes by
Marian J. Holmes

based on readings for
Week 29
(July 16 – 22, 2000)

AIM
To present a wider perspective on 'disability' and show how we all fit into the picture.

'Dignity and compassion for all'

Introduction
In the West, the word 'disability' can evoke many feelings. We hear much about 'equal rights for the disabled', and perhaps find ourselves thinking carefully before we speak on the subject. Jesus had a much broader picture of humanity, and his words went deeper than outward appearances.

● **When a sick or disabled person was brought to Jesus, he treated them with dignity and compassion, taking time to listen and respond to their needs.** He touched them, making them feel wanted instead of outcast; he listened to them, giving them a voice; he spoke to them, offering them, if not physical healing, then certainly inner wholeness, drawing them closer to God.

● **Jesus passed no judgement on people who came to him.** He simply offered them a different way of living. The choice was theirs. To Jesus, being disabled was not connected with 'evil spirits' or paying a penalty for past sins. Each encounter was personalized and designed to reveal God's glory.

● **We all have some form of 'disability'.** We all fall short of what it takes to live the Christian life. Therefore we all need God's word of *shalom*. Only when we recognize our 'disability' before God, and ask his help, can we begin to overcome it. It may never go away, but with God's help we can begin to work with it.

Conclusion Jesus treated people with disabilities exactly like those without: as people with purpose, and precious in God's sight. His belief in the goodness of humanity — God's creation — never faltered, and he gave life to all who met him.

To the preacher. How can you help the congregation to open their minds to see beyond 'society's' view of disability, and hear the words of healing, acceptance and dignity which Jesus speaks to all of us in our 'disability'?

Health for all

Sermon notes by
Martin Lambourne

based on readings for
Week 30
(July 23 – 29, 2000)

Text: 'On the banks, on both sides of the river, there will grow all kinds of trees for food. Their leaves will not wither, nor their fruits fail, but they will bear fresh fruit every month, because the water for them flows from the sanctuary. Their fruit will be for food, and their leaves for healing. '
(Ezekiel 47.12, NRSV)

AIM
To see Jesus as the source of hope for health and wholeness.

Introduction

This vision of the new temple as the source of the river of life is glimpsed again in several places in John's Gospel *(see John 2.19 – 21; John 7.38)*. Health and wholeness have many dimensions. Just as people came to Jesus with their requests for healing, so we come asking:

● **Restore our world.** Our environment is often a comment on those of us who inhabit it. We need help and vision to work for an environment which reflects a respect for the very ground which we use and abuse.

● **Feed our bodies.** Jesus was concerned for the physical well-being of people, old and young. He saw their physical health and strength as an integral part of the salvation of the whole person.

● **Bring us to our senses.** Jesus was also concerned for those whom we see today as mentally unwell. His concern, however, was for our mental attitudes as well, towards those who, for whatever reason, are different from us. For Jesus, there is no difference — we all need to come to our right minds and acknowledge each other's worth.

● **Quench our thirst.** Mark 6.34 shows Jesus overwhelmed by a sense of the people's lack of direction — like sheep without a shepherd. There is a thirst today for 'spiritual' satisfaction, whether it is 'New Age', random mysticism, or other-worldly experiences. Jesus invites us to get in touch with God and discover the water of life; then we will never be thirsty again — or lose our sense of direction!

Conclusion Jesus sees us whole — as individuals, members of a world village, living on a big blue planet. The challenge is to share his vision and enable the waters to flow.

To the preacher. Ground your sermon in the actual 'health problems' (in the widest sense) experienced by the congregation and your neighbourhood.

Bread is for sharing 1

Sermon notes by
Lloyda Fanusie

based on readings for
Week 31
(July 30 – August 5,
2000)

'Turn stones to bread?'

Text: Lifting up his eyes, then, and seeing that a multitude was coming to him, Jesus said to Philip, 'How are we to buy bread, so that these people may eat?' This he said to test him, for he himself knew what he would do. (John 6.5 – 6, RSV)

AIM

To encourage Christians to share their resources for the good of the community and the world at large.

Introduction

How much we value food as a necessity of life! But news and pictures of hungry and emaciated people hurt us; we want to act, to replace the images of starvation and suffering — whether caused by war or by natural disasters — with images of security, adequate food, love, joy and peace. When we hear Jesus' words of love and concern for the needy, we can become transformed, ready for action.

● **Encourage people to look to God for sustenance.** Our gifts and graces/talents come from God as resources which ought to be shared with others, not hoarded for ourselves.

● **Every little counts!** Remember the widow's mite. We may not be able to do much by ourselves, but by joining with others in pressure groups and in giving, we can have an influence.

● **The importance of God's generosity in relation to ours.** Consider the work of charitable organisations like the Red Cross, Tear Fund, Christian Aid — all pro-life. Contrast them with anti-life structures and systems — implements of war, money-led farming methods, pesticides and chemicals which pollute the environment. We must take a stance against destructive systems in order to improve the world.

Conclusion The world needs our moral strength as we make informed decisions on issues like abortion, euthanasia, genetic engineering and self-destructive behaviour — as well as global food policies and over-production. These must be challenged if we are to follow Jesus' instruction to be perfect as our Heavenly Father is perfect.

To the preacher. Jesus teaches us that there is more to life than food. The word of God must succour us — but also challenge us to help all people to live life in all its fullness.

Bread is for sharing 2

Text: **Jesus declared, 'I am the bread of life. He who comes to me will never go hungry, and he who believes in me will never be thirsty.'**

(John 6.35, NIV)

Sermon notes by
Martin Lambourne

based on readings for
Week 32
(August 6 – 12, 2000)

AIM
To see the significance of bread as symbol of both life and life-style.

'The wider significance of bread'

Introduction
When we partake of the one loaf at the Lord's Table, we are not only identifying with Christ whose body was broken for us, but with all for whom Christ died — without exception. This implies that we also have to acknowledge the wider significance of bread.

● **Bread is for nourishment.** We cannot grow without food. No more can we expect to grow in discipleship if we are not giving ourselves a reasonable diet of:

- prayer
- reading
- reflection

to enable us to become mature in the faith rather than stunted and underdeveloped Christians.

● **Bread is for hospitality.** We all need companionship. We were made in the image of God — the Three in One — in communion with each other. It is only in relating to other people that we become human at all. Part of the challenge of the breaking of bread is to recognize our dependency on each other for our human development.

● **Bread is for sharing.** And that means sharing with all — a call to justice. Aileen Khoo from Malaysia, who wrote this week's notes for *Light for Our Path*, reminds us that 'by the year 2000 half of the population of Indonesia will be living below the poverty line due to the economic crisis'. We cannot have half of the world in famine and sit comfortably around any table, let alone the communion table. We must first go and sort out the injustice and then come back!

Conclusion Bread gives us an everyday reminder that our commitment to Christ involves us in a commitment to a life-style which is evident in every aspect of our living with God and with each other.

To the preacher. What suggestions can you make to the congregation to help them be better nourished and increase in hospitality and sharing?

The Church community 1

Sermon notes by
Lloyda Fanusie

based on readings for
Week 33
(August 13 – 19,
2000)

'In the world but not of the world'

Text: **For no other foundation can anyone lay than that which is laid, which is Jesus Christ.**
(1 Corinthians 3.11, RSV)

AIM
To remind people of the authority of Scripture and strengthen their faith in Christ the head of the Church.

Introduction
From its small beginnings in the Middle East, the one, holy, catholic and apostolic Church is now a global entity. Built on the authority of Scripture, it continues to grow, with the risen Christ, its solid foundation stone, as both its head and the proof of our faith. This is the uniqueness of Christianity.

● **The Church is still here!** In spite of the Crusades, vicious wars and in-fighting leading to fragmented denominations, the Church is still here, because its foundation is Christ and all that human beings can do cannot destroy it.

● **We are the Church.** We stand united in our diversity:

- encouraging each other as members of the one Church;
- believing in the One in Three and Three in One God — Creator, Redeemer, Sanctifier;
- spreading the good news of our salvation;
- showing the fruits of the Spirit in our words and actions.

As we plant and build church communities, our lives of fellowship and worship reveal the reality of a thriving Church, rich in its heritage and sacraments.

● **In his service.** Encouraged by Jesus' words that the labourer is worthy of his hire, we offer our services in God's vineyard, to God's glory. We do not seek fame; we avoid dissensions; and we teach and learn in order to increase God's workforce.

● **God's other sheep.** As we face the reality of pluralism, materialism, and secularism, we uphold Jesus' words in John 10.16, that he has other sheep, trying to be tolerant and understanding of others — in the world, but not of the world.

Conclusion Our worship is in vain if we are not spiritually pure, as God requires. This applies also to the Church as a whole; we must fight all abuses inside and outside the Church and preserve the good.

To the preacher. I have described the Church as it should be; what can you and your congregation do to bring the everyday reality of the Church closer to this ideal?

The Church community 2

Sermon notes by
Emmanuel Asante

based on readings for
Week 34
(August 20 – 26,
2000)

'Privilege and
responsibility'

Text: **These things happened to them as examples and were written down as warnings for us, on whom the fulfilment of the ages has come.**

(1 Corinthians 10.11, NIV)

AIM

To learn the spiritual lessons which Israel's past history has for today's believers.

Introduction

In his letter to the Romans, Paul made the point that everything written in the past was written to instruct us, so that as we patiently endure, we might be encouraged to hold fast to our hope in Christ *(Romans 15.4)*. Scripture is intended to teach us what is true, make us realize what is wrong in our lives, and encourage us to do what is right *(2 Timothy 3.16)*. The story of Israel's dealings with God can benefit today's believers in Christ.

● **The privilege of redemption.** The children of Israel had experienced the wonderful privilege of redemption from slavery in Egypt. This experience led them into a covenant relationship with God and with one another. They became the people of God, enjoying his sacramental grace *(verses 2 – 4)*.

● **Privilege without responsibility.** This wonderful privilege called for a corresponding responsibility. As the 'People of God', Israel's responsibility was to thank God by serving him alone in holiness and obedience. But they failed to obey God, to carry out the responsibility that ought to accompany the privileges they enjoyed. They showed ingratitude to God by serving other gods and displeased him by engaging in ritual sex *(verses 5 – 10)*.

● **The past as warning.** Israel's enjoyment of divine privilege and failure to fulfil the accompanying responsibility is a warning to Christians today. We need to draw constant spiritual lessons from the story of Israel as we wait with eager anticipation for the coming of the

Lord. (Give examples of such lessons.)

Conclusion Privilege without a corresponding sense of responsibility amounts to an abuse of divine grace which God will not allow to go unchallenged. This is one of the many lessons we can learn from Israel's story, so that we do not repeat their mistakes.

To the preacher. The means of grace are not ends in themselves; they are a privilege which must be accompanied by a strong sense of responsibility to serve the Lord in the beauty of holiness and obedience.

The Church community 3

Text: I thank God that I speak in tongues more than all of you; nevertheless, in church I would rather speak five words with my mind, in order to instruct others also, than ten thousand words in a tongue. (1 Corinthians 14.18 – 19, NRSV)

Sermon notes by
Catherine Middleton

based on readings for Week 35 (August 27 – September 2, 2000)

AIM
To encourage worshippers to worship in ways that benefit everyone.

'Worship together'

Introduction
Why do people come to worship? To meet with God as individuals? To have 'uplifting' spiritual experiences? Or to share their prayer and praise with others? What do people expect to feel like when the service is ended? Do they expect to have understood all that has been said? Do they expect to feel, perhaps in an indescribable way, closer to God? Do they expect to feel that they have shared in a journey of deepening understanding and commitment with other Christians?

● **The text and its context.** Paul is writing to a congregation in which, as he sees it, heart or spirit, rather than mind, is being given priority. The problem is that while some people are having deeply meaningful individual experiences, these experiences are neither helping the community as a whole nor are they a good way of attracting unbelievers to Christianity. If the mind is not engaged, the spirit will wander off to distant places.

● **Worshipping together.** Paul is not against people having individually meaningful spiritual experiences: he is against them having such experiences in public if others are excluded. Worship should be orderly and comprehensible. Paul singles out the gift of tongues, seeing tongues as a great gift but one to be exercised with discretion. Tongues without interpretation are worth little. Worshippers should gather to give praise, together, to God, not to make public display of their gifts.

● **Understanding is vital if worship is to be a shared experience.**

To the preacher. How is worship led in your church? Is everyone expected to bring something to it? If not, why not?

No generation gap

Sermon notes by
Chris Duffett

based on readings for
Week 36
(September 3 – 9, 2000)

'Happy families'

Text: Do not rebuke an older man harshly, but exhort him as if he were your father. Treat younger men as brothers, older women as mothers, and younger women as sisters, with absolute purity.
(1 Timothy 5.1 – 2, NIV)

AIM
To remind Christians that they are a family.

Introduction
1 Timothy 4.6 – 5.2 gives some background to the relationship between Paul and Timothy. Can the text be applied to the way members of the Church generally relate to each other? Highlight some of the possible barriers between people: class, age, race, etc. Jesus is what every Christian has in common and the basis of our relationship with each other. Jesus changes us to be...

● **Brothers and sisters with Jesus.** Emphasize the changes that happen to a person becoming a Christian. We become 'heirs of God' *(Romans 8.17)*, 'dearly loved children' *(Ephesians 5.1)*, every one of us a priest *(Revelation 1.6)*. When we become Christians we become brothers and sisters together.

● **An example to our communities.** Our relationships with each other are a witness to the people in our communities (the verse about being a light to the world may be applicable, *Matthew 5.14*). If others see the Church living as a family, they will want to share it and will come and join our family too.

Conclusion Talk about how families should relate to each other, and give an example from your own or someone else's family. Stress again that this is what the Church should be like, young and old living together. There should be no generation gap between the oldest and youngest; family brings them together.

To the preacher. Could you interview two Christians from different generations to explore the theme that Jesus brings people together as family? Also, share some stories of how families function together and relate these stories to how the Church family should treat each other, i.e. eating together, spending time with each other etc...

No one excluded

Sermon notes by
Chris Duffett

based on readings for
**Week 37
(September 10 – 16,
2000)**

*'Actions speak
louder than
words'*

Text: **This is how we know what love is: Jesus Christ laid down his life for us. And we ought to lay down our lives for our brothers. If anyone has material possessions and sees his brother in need but has no pity on him, how can the love of God be in him? Dear children, let us not love with words or tongue but with actions and in truth.**

(1 John 3.16 – 18, NIV)

AIM
To encourage the demonstration of the gospel in the community.

Introduction
St Francis of Assisi once said, 'Preach the gospel always — sometimes use words'. Give an example of a Christian you know who has had a profound effect through demonstrating the gospel, e.g. Mother Teresa. Stress that we all need to demonstrate God's love to people so as to ensure that no one is excluded from the love God has for them. People need to see the love of God in the following ways:

● **Being an example of Jesus to others.** *(Verse 16)* What does Jesus laying down his life for you mean to you? If you can, tell the story of a local hero, from your community or from the national papers, who put their life on the line for someone else. This is what Jesus wants us to do: to love with our whole lives.

● **The way we live.** *(Verse 17)* Talk about the importance of giving to others.

- Helping others pleases God: 'And do not forget to do good and to share with others, for with such sacrifices God is pleased' *(Hebrews 13.16)*.

- Giving to others shows the love of God to people around us, not only to the people we help.

● **The way we love.** Emphasize verse 18. Talk about

practical ways the Church can love in actions and truth in the community.

Conclusion Wallis writes, 'People should be able to look at the way we live and begin to understand what the gospel is about. Our life must tell them who Jesus is and what he cares about' (*J Wallis, The Call To Conversion, Lion 1981, p. 108*).

To the preacher. Are there areas in your life where you need to love in action and truth rather than words?

Forgetting self

Text: **Jesus called the crowd and his disciples to him. 'If anyone wants to come with me,' he told them, 'he must forget self, carry his cross, and follow me.'**
(Mark 8.34, GNB)

Sermon notes by
David Huggett

based on readings for
Week 38
(September 17-23,
2000)

AIM
To help people to assess their own self-worth.

'Follow me'

Introduction
Don't underestimate your value — after all, Christ valued you so highly that he died for you.

● **We need to know self.** Do we spend too much time trying to hide what we are really like from ourselves and others? An honest and balanced self-appraisal is vital so that we are aware of our strengths and weaknesses. Other people can help us to do this if they are also prepared to be honest, and psychological tools like Myers-Briggs and the Enneagram can also be useful.

● **We need to accept self.** Some of what we discover about ourselves we will not like very much. But we need to learn to accept ourselves and stop blaming God for who we are. And then we need to go on to accept what we can become if we allow God to take over. Every one of us has hidden potential — look for it and accept it.

● **We need to forget self.** This does not mean crushing or repressing ourselves and our feelings. Christianity has often been depicted as grim duty when it should be the delighted acknowledgement of all that God can do with us. But reaching out for that potential means being prepared to forget or to deny ourselves whatever might deflect us from what God wants us to be. If we focus on the wealth, popularity, status and success that advertisers tell us are essential to a fulfilled life, we shall miss the real purpose of living.

Conclusion Jesus gives us the supreme example. Because his purpose was to bring salvation to this world, he was prepared to forget himself even to the point of submitting to death in order to achieve this aim.

To the preacher. This verse is not to be taken in isolation but in the context of Jesus' awareness of his mission.

Honouring marriage

Sermon notes by
Heather Ward

based on readings for
Week 39
(September 24 – 30,
2000)

'Loyal to Christ, loyal to each other'

Text: **Many women do noble things ... but a woman who fears the LORD is to be praised.**
(Proverbs 31.29 – 30, NIV)

AIM
To show that the person who gives worship and honour to God adds a greater quality to their marriage.

Introduction
Today we live in a world where sex is important, but many people have little respect for faithfulness in marriage, or even for getting married, and children may be brought up without the support of two parents. The idea of religious worship, and the meaning of the love of God, is often scorned rather than honoured. As Christians we should challenge ourselves: how do we honour God through our marriage? Do we encourage our children so that they too may know God's love in their lives? Or if we are single, how do we live satisfied lives without dishonouring someone else's marriage?

- **The Wife of Noble Character.** This is the heading for Proverbs 31.10 – 31 in the NIV. She is pictured as an outstanding woman, extremely hard-working, providing for her family, servants, the poor and the needy with energy, enjoyment and wise judgement, gaining respect from her husband, children and the community. This is attributed to the fact that she honours God.

- **Marriage today.** Picture a marriage today in your own community. Probably both partners go out to work, and they may share the work in the home, the care of the children and the finances. Or, by contrast, you could picture the marriage where the husband still leaves all the work in the home to the wife.

- **Christ in marriage.** Discuss the need for Christ in the home, and the way in which Bible reading, prayer and church fellowship can strengthen a marriage. Loyalty to Christ can bring loyalty to one another.

To the preacher. This theme could be developed as a normal sermon, or it could be presented as a short drama, presenting bad and good examples, followed by a brief conclusion. If you are giving illustrations from life, take care that people do not think that you are 'picking on' a particular person. Proverbs can make people think, but it is the hearers who must challenge themselves.

Sharing suffering 1

Text: **Then Satan answered the LORD: 'Does Job fear God for nothing? ... You have blessed the work of his hands, and his possessions have increased in the land. But stretch out your hand now, and touch all that he has, and he will curse you to your face.'** (Job 1.9 - 11, NRSV)

Sermon notes by
Kate Hughes

based on readings for
Week 40
(October 1 – 7, 2000)

AIM
To remind the congregation that our relationship with God, the giver, is more important than his gifts.

'The giver is more important than the gifts'

Introduction

God had been generous to Job. But, contrary to what Satan thinks, it is his relationship with God, the giver, which is more important to Job than all his wealth. This is what he argues with God about, not the loss of his possessions. Can the same be said of us?

● **What's in it for us?** Of course, being a Christian brings many spiritual benefits — and sometimes material benefits as well. And God's greatest gift to us is salvation — being in a right relationship with him. But we are on the wrong track if we are always adding up the benefits and asking, 'What's in it for us? Is it worth our while?'

● **The gifts or the giver?** This attitude misses the point of Christianity. God is not there to give us what we think we need; he will give us what he knows we need. This may include a good job, a nice house, beautiful children, many possessions. Or it may include sickness, unemployment, poverty and constant struggle. It is not which gifts we receive which is most important, but what builds up our relationship with the giver.

● **Learning to share in God's life.** Our task is not to persuade God to share in our life and give us what we see as the right things, but to learn to share in God's life — a life which, because of human sin, includes suffering and the cross. In the words of Romans 8.39, nothing 'in all creation' — not possessions or loss of possessions — 'will be able to separate us from the love of God in Christ Jesus'. So why reject him because he knows better than us what we really need?

To the preacher. God does, of course, give all of us many gifts — but we need to focus on the giver, while thanking him for the gifts.

Sharing suffering 2

Text: 'Snares are all around you, and sudden terrors make you afraid.' (Job 22.10, NJB)

Sermon notes by
Mike Pennington

based on readings for
Week 41
(October 8 – 14, 2000)

'Do what you can'

AIM
To find ways of not feeling useless when facing others' suffering.

● **Rewards and punishments?** We are wrong if we see pain and disaster, ease or prosperity as God's rewards and punishments. Disaster may result from human behaviour: building houses at the foot of a volcano, or driving a car recklessly. We must live within the limits of creation.

● **People's unexplained suffering.** We question the justice of suffering when we encounter people who are terminally ill, or an unexpected family death, particularly of a young person or baby. How can we deal with this?

● **Feeling helpless.** Non-Christian sufferers often expect us to give a satisfactory answer. But we too feel helpless when we, and the doctors and nurses, have done all we can, yet the patient still suffers, or when someone loses their job, or has their home flooded. Our words and resources are inadequate, but we must realize that we are not all-powerful — we are not God, only his agents and channels of his love.

● **Do what we can.** Even if more is needed, we must do what we can *(Luke 17.10)*, 'being' perhaps rather than 'doing', sharing the suffering in very simple and practical ways: holding a hand, moistening dry lips, washing up, praying with or for the person — being there, possibly for a long time, watching in silence through the night. Jesus teaches that such actions are directed towards him *(Matthew 25.40)*, and that he is with us, to the end of time *(Matthew 28.20)*.

Conclusion In the face of suffering, we must do all we can, but not over-estimate what we can do or provide, nor under-estimate what we can do in other directions.

To the preacher. People often feel guilty that they cannot meet the needs of a sufferer. Be positive about what they can do, not negative about situations beyond them. Speak at a personal level — don't engage in problems of world-wide famines which even national governments cannot relieve!

Sharing suffering 3

Sermon notes by
Mike Pennington

based on readings for
Week 42
(October 15 – 21, 2000)

'Getting ready for anything'

Text: **'Despite my groans, his hand is just as heavy.'**
(Job 23.2, NJB)

AIM
To explore the implications of one's own suffering.

Introduction
In texts such as Colossians 3.12–14, Christians are exhorted to care, serve, love, etc. This defines our ministry to someone in need, following the example of Jesus *(Mark 10.45)*. But if we are the person in need, how do we react to our own suffering, and to people helping us? If our home is destroyed, or we lose our job, our baby dies, or we suffer physical pain, what can we do about it?

● **Pain.** People in excruciating pain often retreat into a shell, shutting out other people. But we can learn to let hurt of any kind flow over us, not allowing it to penetrate our depths, only our body. This is a technique which develops with practice, even when powerful drugs are useless.

● **Death.** We all die. Apart from the pain often involved in the process, does death hurt the person dying — or just their relatives and friends?

● **Loss.** Job's reaction to loss was 'I don't know what I've done to deserve this' *(1.14 – 19)*. Jesus' answer is found in Luke 13.4. Statistical laws apply to all, including Christians — why should disaster not strike me?

● **Blame.** Insurance companies describe disasters that no one could foresee or prevent as 'Acts of God'. A common reaction is 'Who can I blame?' Some people blame God; others sue someone, finding justice in financial compensation.

● **We are not God.** God is not required to explain his actions to us. In the end, all Job could say was, 'I retract what I have said, and repent in dust and ashes' *(42.6)*, submitting to his will and wisdom as Jesus did in Gethsemane *(Matthew 26.39)*.

Conclusion The resources of Christian faith enable us to address our own suffering, deserved or not. We can prepare beforehand, building up our skills and resources like a first aid kit.

To the preacher. These notes will stand alone or make a pair with last week's. The ethics of using litigation to deal with blame and anger need a separate sermon — don't try to cover it here!

Celebration

Text: You cause the grass to grow for the cattle, and plants for people to use, to bring forth food from the earth, and wine to gladden the human heart, oil to make the face shine, and bread to strengthen the human heart.   **(Psalm 104.14 - 15, NRSV)**

Sermon notes by
Kate Hughes

based on readings for
Week 43
(October 22 – 28,
2000)

AIM
To show that, in spite of disasters, we can celebrate God's creation.

'God provides all we need'

Introduction
When we think of creation today, we tend to focus on the disasters: the famines and drought in Africa, the floods in Bangladesh, the destruction of the rainforest in South America. But we can also celebrate God's creation.

● **Natural resources.** The ability of nature to regenerate is amazing. Few ecological and environmental disasters are irreversible or final — given the will and the resources to tackle them. It is human sin which all too often creates the disasters in the first place and allows them to become final.

● **Food for the earth.** In spite of the disasters, we can celebrate God's creation, because the majority of people in the world do get fed every day, even if we need to distribute the earth's resources much more fairly. God has provided enough food — but we have to co-operate with him so that everyone gets enough.

● **Joy for the human heart.** God's creation not only supplies our basic needs; it also gives us the 'extras' which can make human life so rich: a variety of food and drink, art, music, writing, science, community, and so on — symbolized in the psalm by wine and oil.

● **Strength for the human spirit.** Bread, as the basic food for many people, is used in the Bible as a symbol of all God's provision for his people. God's creation can provide all that we need for our bodies, minds and spirits, and our trust in him and his provision is the source of our strength.

To the preacher. Please avoid any suggestion that the connection between human sin and environmental disaster is one of punishment! Our God is not like that!

Protest

Text: It was not for any fault on the part of creation that it was made unable to attain its purpose, it was made so by God; but creation still retains the hope of being freed, like us, from its slavery to decadence, to enjoy the same freedom and glory as the children of God.   (Romans 8.20 – 21, JB)

Sermon notes by
Philip Wetherell

based on readings for
Week 44
(October 29 –
November 4, 2000)

AIM

To show that our special relationship with God implies responsibility for all creation.

Introduction

'Redeeming all creation'

People regard the world around them in different ways according to their culture and situation: a tourist and a cattle farmer in rural Africa will see different things when they watch a lion; a road builder and an archaeologist will view a piece of land in crowded Europe from different points of view. Each will have a different priority. What is our responsibility when we have been told to conquer and master the world *(Genesis 1.28)*? There is no biblical mandate for the idea that any part of creation is disposable, or that any part has absolute power. 'To master' does not mean 'to destroy'.

● **The freeing of creation.** The whole world has been cursed for human sin *(Genesis 3.17)* — stripped, polluted and exploited. But salvation will include cursed creation, freed from wrongful human domination and from slavery to human greed.

● **Part of the covenant.** Links between the elements of God's creation are enshrined in a covenant with all humanity — Noah preserves all created things, not just those useful to humans, and God promises never again to curse the earth because of human sin *(Genesis 8.15 – 22)*.

● **Our responsibility.** We have a special relationship with God, and our behaviour affects the whole of creation. Therefore, we have a part in its future, and in ensuring it does not revert to chaos. Redemption in Christ is promised, but is not reserved for humans *(Romans 8.21)*.

To the preacher. It is difficult for any congregation to take on the world, to know what to do about global issues. Is there a local issue about which you could all take action, and through which change could happen?

Call for action

Sermon notes by
Peter Tongeman

based on readings for
Week 45
(November 5 – 11,
2000)

'Religion and life-style'

Text: **What does the LORD require of you? To act justly and to love mercy and to walk humbly with your God.** **(Micah 6.8, NIV)**

AIM
To show how obedience to God's requirements affects the quality of daily life.

Introduction

Micah complained about the people of Israel. There was a discrepancy between their religion and their life-style. They worshipped a just God but acted unjustly; welcomed God's mercy but showed little themselves. If a scientist treats his neighbour badly, his scientific ability is unimpaired. But if a Christian treats his neighbour badly, his religious profession is seriously damaged, because acknowledging God, following Jesus, involves care for people as well as worship of God. Love for God and love for neighbour are inseparable.

● **Right behaviour.** Explore what it means to 'act justly' in your situation. Who are your neighbours? What should you do, or not do, to live up to God's standard? Consider this in the light of five of the ten commandments *(Exodus 20.13 – 17)*.

● **Good relationships.** 'Love mercy.' Justice sends a person to prison for a crime committed; mercy cares for his family and helps him to recover. Mercy is undeserved kindness. It is what Jesus showed to others, and how God deals with us. It leads to forgiveness and reconciliation. It is essential for good relationships.

- **A godly life.** 'Walk humbly with God'. Here is the source of strength to attempt God's requirements. 'Walk' implies movement, progress. 'Humbly' implies submission to his will, the recognition of our utter dependence on him. 'With God' suggests fellowship, daily companionship. These are the ingredients of a godly life.

Conclusion There will always be a gap between the ideal and the actual, but we should not be complacent. We are called to strive for the best and the highest with the strength that God provides.

To the preacher. Examine your own life-style in the light of today's verse. Remember you are as much in need of God's mercy and strength as your congregation.

Hope

Text: Praise the LORD, O my soul. I will praise the LORD all my life; I will sing praise to my God as long as I live. **(Psalm 146.1 – 2, NIV)**

Sermon notes by
Elina Templin

based on readings for
Week 46
(November 12 – 18, 2000)

AIM
To encourage people to celebrate the creative power of God's Word.

- **The joy of celebrating.** Praise the LORD, O my soul! Newspapers tell us that people do not buy 'good news', only reports of disasters, tragedies, murders, etc. (although the Gospel, literally translated as Good News, seems to have sold quite well). When things go badly for us, we are quick to cry out to God, but how often do we celebrate God-with-us, Emmanuel? It is the devil's work to lie — to fill our lives with darkness and despair. Against this, Christians affirm the 'truly eucharistic life' of praise and thanksgiving. The purpose of our lives is to 'glorify God and to enjoy him forever'(*Westminster Confession*).

- **The need for protest.** Developing countries with little have a great deal to teach those with much: appreciation of scarce natural resources, a simpler life-style, the priority

'Behold! I make all things new'

of human relationships. Their voices must be heard — even become our collective conscience — so that we are prepared to share God's creation more equitably.

● **The call for action.** Talk about sin as 'mutilation of life'. Wherever life is mutilated, human beings are devalued, and sickness and poverty keep people from becoming fully human — there Christians must be involved, to bring in the healing love of Christ.

● **Hope.** Christian hope is costly. It only comes when we 'stand fast', facing the darkness head on, and hold to God's promise of redemption. This hope can never be in vain because it rests on the creative power of God's Word.

Conclusion So we celebrate and give thanks that all things are possible through this Word spoken in Jesus Christ — to raise up, make new, and redeem the lost things of our lives.

To the preacher. Give personal examples of lives transformed by the power of the gospel. Your own?

Prayer 1

Sermon Notes by
Peter Tongeman

based on readings for
Week 47
(November 19 – 25, 2000)

'Blind and deaf'

Text: 'You have seen many things, but have paid no attention; your ears are open, but you hear nothing.' **(Isaiah 42.20, NIV)**

AIM
To show the dangers of ignoring or rejecting the principles for living which God has provided, and the wisdom of adopting them.

Introduction
Isaiah the prophet reminded the Israelites, who had been defeated and forced to live in exile in Babylon, that they had brought their plight upon themselves. It was because 'they would not follow [God's] ways' *(verse 24)*. Not until they learned their lesson would the nation return to normality.

● **Blind.** We are 'blind' when we see resources exploited

and the environment polluted by greed, yet do nothing about it. Such short-term gain for a few causes the majority to suffer. By paying little attention, allowing it to continue unrestrained, we abuse God's gifts and mortgage the future of our unborn children.

● **Deaf.** We are 'deaf' when we hear the cry of the poor, the pleas of the hungry, the protests of the homeless, the appeal of those unjustly treated, yet do nothing about it. To seek only our own comfort, regardless of others' needs, is to 'turn a deaf ear' and incur God's judgement.

● **Seeing and hearing.** God has provided all we need for life *(Psalm 65.9 – 13)*. When his gifts are abused it is our duty to take action. God complained of Eli that he 'failed to restrain' his sons in their sinful ways *(1 Samuel 3.13)*. Careful attention to biblical principles, and readiness to put them into practice, prevents calamity caused by selfishness, greed and indifference.

Conclusion We bring judgement on ourselves by disobedience. But God does not forsake us *(verse 16)*. With our co-operation he 'makes the rough places smooth' and 'turns the darkness into light'.

To the preacher. In what ways are you and your congregation blind or deaf to God's guidelines for living? What action could be taken to put things right?

Prayer 2

Text: 'Is not my house right with God? Has he not made with me an everlasting covenant, arranged and secured in every part? Will he not bring to fruition my salvation and grant me my every desire?

(2 Samuel 23.5, NIV)

Sermon notes by
Tom Arthur

based on readings for
Week 48
(November 26 –
December 2, 2000)

AIM
To discern God's faithfulness even in defeat.

'God's providence continues'

Introduction

David seems to be certain of God's continuing favour to his royal house. By contrast, the sermon might set out some challenging questions. We are reluctant simply to affirm the royal covenant, because the prophets condemn those who presume on God's favour. We know about the cross, and about the state of the Church at the turn of the second millennium. How do we discern God's continuing favour, in the face of what seems to be the real story of continuing defeat?

● **God's promise to the house of David is very specific.** God's promises of life, freedom and land to his people are here interpreted within the context of divine favour to a particular dynasty. What are we to make of this? Institutions of governance, dynasties, empires and nations come and go and evolve throughout history.

● **David's kingdom was sustained by God's grace, not by David.** David's words are thanksgiving, not arrogance. If our communities are constituted by the grace of God, not our own power, then we are not our own — as David himself had to learn through bitter experience. We have certain obligations to live and work as God's people. What happens to us when we forget that we are sustained by grace? What happens to the way we treat one another, other nations, the earth, the seas, the air? Are failures and disasters God's responsibility or ours?

● **God's favour continues.** How does God's favour continue, despite our wandering away from God? God's royal covenant with the house of David says that all governments everywhere are sustained by grace, that God provides the means for people to live righteously and even prosperously. Nations will continue to come and go; realizing this fact gives us a proper, God-centred perspective. God's providence will continue, overriding the collapse of particular historical institutions, but giving hope to those who open their ways to God's grace.

To the preacher. You may be able to use illustrations from the history of your own country and church.

God's Kingdom

Text: 'It is not anyone who says to me, "Lord, Lord", who will enter the kingdom of Heaven, but the person who does the will of my Father in heaven.' (Matthew 7.21, NJB)

Sermon notes by
Paul Duffett

based on readings for
Week 49
(December 3 – 9,
2000)

AIM
To show that God's activity in the world includes calling people to co-operate with him in 'Kingdom building'.

'God loves his world and seeks to make it his realm'

Introduction
In the Lord's prayer Jesus taught us to ask God to bring in his Kingdom now. Can we be part of that prayer?

● **Where is God's Kingdom?** Draw or describe the world as a circle with a cross in the middle. Around the cross is a smaller circle, filled with tiny crosses; this is the Church. Where is God's Kingdom — in the big circle, which includes the cross, the Church and the whole world? Or just in the smaller circle of the Church?

● **In the world?** Those who say, 'Lord, Lord' but do nothing are declaring that God's Kingdom is superficial, a nice 'extra' which has no real effect on the rest of life.

● **In the Church?** On the other hand, some people see the Kingdom as the same as the Church, an ark to keep Christians safe from the wicked world where Satan reigns. The fellowship is everything and what happens in society has nothing to do with them — or God's Kingdom.

● **The Kingdom builders.** Draw or describe little crosses all over the larger circle of the 'world', some alone, some in small groups. These are Christians who gather for worship but then scatter to build God's Kingdom where they work and live.

Conclusion Jesus drew several pictures of 'the Kingdom': as soil in which seed is planted and grows and produces fruit *(Luke 8)*; or as a precious treasure *(Matthew 13.44 – 45)*. Working for the Kingdom is the number one activity of those who are God's children. The Kingdom is also a 'net' *(Matthew 13.47 – 50)*, and sorting out who is in it and who is outside is something for the future. Our calling is to work in the Kingdom now.

To the preacher. Where is God's Kingdom apart from the Christian Church?

God's messengers

Sermon notes by
Paul Duffett

based on readings for
Week 50
(December 10 – 16,
2000)

'God speaks
and means to
be heard'

Text: 'Look, I shall send my messenger to clear a way before me.' **(Malachi 3.1, NJB)**

AIM
To show that God speaks his message through people in the Bible and today through us.

Introduction
Christmas cards have begun to arrive. They bring messages from people we know and sometimes this is the only contact we have with them during the whole year. If a letter is enclosed, we receive all sorts of information about them and their families.

● **Preparing the way.** Some messengers play a vital role in preparing for the coming of an important person or event — for example, the athlete who carries the flame into the arena before the Olympic Games can begin. Or the people who put palms and branches on the road in front of Jesus when he rode into Jerusalem.

● **The Christmas messengers.** The first Christmas was announced by a number of messengers:

- the angel (meaning 'messenger') Gabriel
- as a result of his message, Zechariah, who gave his own message in the 'Benedictus' *(Luke 1.68 – 79)*
- Mary, who, when she received Gabriel's message, visited Elizabeth, who had a message for her; then Mary gave her own message in the 'Magnificat' *(Luke 1.46 – 55)*
- John the Baptist with his powerful message.

● **The message.** Messages are meant to be heard and make a difference! When Jesus was born, the angel told the shepherds: 'I bring you news of great joy — a joy to be shared by the whole people.' Jesus, the Word of God incarnate, is a message of great joy. His coming changes everything.

Conclusion If we receive the message, it is bound to affect our lives, and inevitably we become messengers in our turn. What do others make of who we are, what we do, and what we say?

To the preacher. Someone once said, 'If we have joy in our hearts, we should not forget to tell our faces'! Does your joy in Christ make you a messenger to others?

Power to change

Text: John declared before them all, 'I baptise you with water, but someone is coming, who is more powerful than me ... he will baptise you with the Holy Spirit and fire.' (Luke 3.16, NJB)

Sermon notes by
Paul Duttett

based on readings for
Week 51
(December 17 – 23,
2000)

AIM
To help people to be more aware of God the Holy Spirit within them, giving them power to change.

Introduction
The only sign of growth is change. Think of creation and the changes which take place in nature all the time: the seed into the flower, the egg into the bird, the caterpillar into the butterfly, the egg into the foetus, etc. Think, too, of the changes taking place all the time in society, some of which bring improvements to the human race, while others do great damage. What is true of creation is also true of the spiritual realm.

● **The Holy Spirit as fire.** Fire purifies as well as destroys. Fire brings heat to help us. Fire changes water to steam, supplies power for electricity, makes steel in a furnace, produces gold. Is that why the Spirit appeared on the

'God can make stones into children!'

apostles at Pentecost as fire? They were to be purified and become agents of power for others.

● **The Holy Spirit as personal.** The fruits of the Spirit are personal love, joy, peace, etc. *(Galatians 5.22 – 23)*, and personal communion with God in prayer. The Spirit gives gifts and graces to be used in the personal service of others.

Conclusion We need to change! We all know this, but change is often uncomfortable. It is easier to stay as we are. But change is happening all around us anyway: We can go with it, or dig in our heels and resist. The Holy Spirit is gentle with us, a power of love to lead us deeper into life with God. The sign of the Spirit's coming — baptism — is for the whole of us, body, mind and spirit.

To the preacher. If you can, give some examples of change led by the Spirit from your own experience.

Come and worship 1

Sermon notes by
Paul Duffett

based on readings for
Week 52
(December 24 – 30, 2000)

'Wonder beyond words'

Text: **Mary ... treasured all these things and pondered them in her heart. And the shepherds went back glorifying and praising God for all they had heard and seen.** **(Luke 2.19 – 20, NJB)**

AIM
To demonstrate that spirituality is a balance of 'Mary' and 'the shepherds'.

● **Mary.** Mary and Joseph share a secret. Joseph has come to accept that what Mary told him is true: the Holy Spirit has caused Mary to conceive. Now God puts the pieces of the jigsaw together: a census means that they must go to Bethlehem, King David's birthplace, where Micah says the Messiah will be born. Mary and Joseph trust each other and obey God. God uses secular events and places — he is not a 'religious' God! The birth of Mary's baby appears humble but is in fact an extraordinary event. Mary's heart is open to God; she prays and thinks, seeing the significance of what is happening. Like her, we need to use our minds prayerfully, to search the Scriptures and see how God is acting in our lives.

● **The shepherds.** God makes this 'private' family affair public. The public are working men going about their daily (nightly) duties. Again, the setting is not religious. They are overwhelmed by the light, what they are told, and the worshipping angels. But they are also thrilled and can't wait to get to Bethlehem. 'Anyone seen a baby in a manger?' (I wonder who was looking after the sheep?) When they find him, they blurt out their story. They had seen many lambs born, and now here was a 'lamb of God'. What next? They remember their sheep and go (running?) back, their praise brimming over. People who heard about them were 'astonished' *(verse 18)*.

Conclusion Michael Cassidy, a Christian leader in South Africa, describes the Christian life as a wheel. The hub is the Father, Son and Holy Spirit. From the hub there are four 'spokes': prayer, the Bible, fellowship and service — telling and doing. The rim of the wheel is the 'balanced Christian in action'. We need both the private witness of Mary, at the hub, and the public witness of the shepherds, running out to the rim.

To the preacher. Imagine yourself at the manger and take part in the action, both as Mary and as the shepherds.

Come and worship 2

Text: **To the One seated on the throne and to the Lamb, be all praise, honour, glory and power, for ever and ever.** **(Revelation 5.13b, NJB)**

Sermon notes by
Paul Duffett
based on reading for
Week 53
(December 31, 2000
– January 6, 2001)

AIM
To show that worship is the sum of all activity.

Introduction
In the marriage service in the *Book of Common Prayer* of the Church of England, the bridegroom says to the bride:

'Just as I am, O Lamb of God, I come'

'With my body I thee [you] worship'. What does this mean? Whatever else it means, it has something to do with love and dedication. That is what worship is about.

● **God on a throne.** Most people know that only the most important rulers are 'enthroned'. They may be human, but their title and position give them a unique place and demand or call out homage and respect (and sometimes admiration and affection) from those they rule. Although the writer of Revelation pictures God as such a ruler, he knows that God is unlike anyone else. There is no way, except an inadequate picture, to describe God's beauty, wonder and awesomeness. God is beyond time, the creator and sustainer of life.

● **The Lamb in the middle.** But in 'the middle of the throne' *(verse 6)* there is a lamb. What is it doing here, this symbol of innocence? It had a place in Jewish worship and Scripture as a symbol of offering (expand), and John the Baptist called Jesus 'the Lamb of God', because at God's heart there is the offering and outpouring of self-giving love. At the manger, God becomes innocent humanity. His mercy and forgiveness are an essential part of his power and glory; he is both King and Lamb.

Conclusion Paul exhorts the Christians in Rome to worship with the words 'remembering the mercies of God' *(Romans 12.1)*. As we reflect upon and recall those mercies, we are bound to respond. Paul goes on to say that intelligent worship means offering ourselves to God, for God. When we offer our heart, all living becomes a form of worship.

To the preacher. Read Revelation chapters 4 and 5 and reflect how they depict worship as of the Father and the Son, in the Spirit.

FINDING OUR WAY TOGETHER series

- For leaders of house fellowships, Bible study groups and worship groups

- Lively and provocative notes, offering a unique opportunity to explore world issues and contemporary themes in the light of the Bible

- Including background notes, ways to lead small groups, contemporary stories, activities for adults, questions for discussion, suggestions for prayer and ideas for further action

- Based on the same passages and themes as *Words for Today*, *Light for our Path* and *Preachers' Handbook*

Books 1, 2 and 3: UK price £6.00 each

IBRA

Order through your IBRA representative or from the appropriate address on page 80.

INDEX OF BIBLE TEXTS REFERRED TO

ABOUT THE AUTHORS

Tom Arthur, an American Presbyterian, served three churches in Cardiff and is now minister of Weoley Hill United Reformed Church in Birmingham, England.

Emmanuel Asante is an ordained minister of the Methodist Church in Ghana and teaches theology at Trinity College, Accra.

Peter Cotterell is a Uniting Church parish minister in Wynyard, Tasmania. He has also served on local, regional, state and national committees and was Moderator of the Synod of Tasmania for 1993–5.

Rodney Dreyer is an Anglican priest from South Africa working in the Church of England as Vicar of Hawkhurst in the Diocese of Canterbury, and also as a facilitator and consultant in the field of theological education.

Chris Duffett is a community worker for a Baptist church in Chester, England, with a particular concern for evangelism, the homeless and young people.

Paul Duffett, an Anglican priest, worked in the Diocese of Zululand for sixteen years. Returning to England, he was rector of several parishes and has recently retired.

Lloyda Fanusie, from Sierra Leone, is a Methodist Local Preacher in London, currently engaged in Racism Awareness Workshops.

Isaiah Gaddala is an Assistant Professor of Homiletics at Union Biblical Seminary, Pune, India, and also travels widely in India conducting revivals, retreats and workshops.

Marian Holmes is a musician and currently Director of Music at a school in England, after thirteen years spent as a member of an Anglican religious community, travelling extensively in the USA and England teaching on worship and worship leading.

David Huggett is a Baptist minister who has been involved in adult Christian education. Currently he is the Secretary of the Western Baptist Association in South West England.

Kate Hughes worked for the Church in Southern Africa for 14 years and is now a freelance editor and writer working from her home in an Urban Priority Area council estate in Coventry, England.

Estela Lamas is a Methodist who lives in Portugal, where she is deeply involved with women's issues; she is currently preparing a PhD thesis in theology on 'The Pastoral Work of Women'.

Martin Lambourne is a Baptist minister who, after pastoral ministries in England, is now Director of Resource Development for the National Christian Education Council.

Catherine Middleton, a minister of the United Reformed Church, is Acting Chaplain and Director of Ministerial Education and Training at Mansfield College, Oxford.

Supriyo Mukherjee is an Anglican priest, ordained in the Church of North India and now working in England as Diocesan Adviser for Community Relations and Inter-faith for Coventry and Team Vicar of Coventry East Team Ministry.

Ngozi Nkeke, from Nigeria, now lives in England and works in the voluntary sector, finding ways to tackle social exclusion among the most disadvantaged groups in society.

Valerie Ogden served the United Church of Zambia as a Methodist minister for 5 years and is now back in England on the staff of the Wolverhampton Trinity Circuit.

Joy Pegg worked as a missionary linguist in Papua New Guinea. Back in Britain, she gained a Masters degree in Old Testament and currently teaches part time while caring for her family.

Mike Pennington is a retired Anglican priest who served in deprived areas in the north of England and as a school and hospital chaplain, and is still active in church work in Newcastle upon Tyne, England.

Judith Rossall is the minister of Guildford Methodist Church and the Free Church chaplain for both the University of Surrey and a small local hospital.

Allen Smith was ordained as an Anglican priest in South Africa in 1990 and now has a parish in Queenstown in the Eastern Cape.

Jember Teferra is an Ethiopian who has worked for seventeen years in the poorest slums of Addis Ababa, helping to alleviate urban poverty and promoting a philosophy known as the integrated holistic approach.

Elina Templin is Canadian by birth but studied theology and was ordained as a Presbyterian minister in South Africa. She has recently returned to Canada, where she continues both her parish ministry and her work as a music teacher.

Peter Tongeman is a retired Baptist minister. He was President of the Baptist Union of Great Britain for a year and is now a freelance writer and poet.

Philip Wadham is a priest in the Anglican Church of Canada and a Regional Mission Co-ordinator for Latin America and the Caribbean. He has worked in Western Canada, Ecuador and England.

Heather Ward is a Methodist Local Preacher who has worked as a teacher in Zimbabwe and as a residential social worker in a hostel for people with learning difficulties.

Philip Wetherell works as the administrator of a development organization working in Zambia, and as a freelance writer and consultant. He has also worked as a missionary teacher in Namibia and for the United Society for the Propagation of the Gospel.

INTERNATIONAL BIBLE READING ASSOCIATION

– a worldwide service of the National Christian Education Council
at work in five continents.

HEADQUARTERS

1020 Bristol Road
Selly Oak
Birmingham
Great Britain
B29 6LB
and the following agencies

AUSTRALIA

Uniting Education (previously The Joint Board of Christian Education)
PO Box 1245 (65 Oxford Street)
Collingwood
Victoria 3066

GHANA

IBRA Secretary
PO Box 919
Accra

INDIA

All India Sunday School Association
PO Box 2099
Secunderabad – 500 003
Andhra Pradesh

NEW ZEALAND

Epworth Bookshop
PO Box 6133, Te Aro
75 Taranaki Street
Wellington 6035

NIGERIA

IBRA Representative
PMB 5298
Ibadan

SOUTH AND CENTRAL AFRICA

IBRA Representative
Box 1176
Sedgefield 6573